The JUNETEENTH Story

CELEBRATING THE END OF SLAVERY IN THE UNITED STATES

Written by Alliah L. Agostini

Illustrated by Sawyer Cloud

becker&mayer! kids

To my grandparents,
Judson Travels Price Jr. and Frances May Taliaferro Price,
and generations of our ancestors.
It is an honor to stand on your shoulders.

The story of Juneteenth started hundreds of years before it was ever celebrated.

On July 4, 1776, Independence Day, America broke away from British rule, and was finally able to bask in the light of freedom . . .

But not everyone who lived there was that fortunate.

For what would span over 300 years, more than 400,000 African people were stolen from their homes and made to help build the country that became this "free" America. Though some tried to fight back, they and many of their descendants were enslaved, brutally forced to work for no pay, and denied their basic rights.

They could not eat what they wanted to eat.

They could not play when they wanted to play.

They could not live how they wanted to live.

And Independence Day did not free them. It would take eighty-nine more years until enslaved people, too, would be free.

Glimmers of freedom appeared state by state in the new, independent America.

Vermont was the first to free, or "emancipate," its enslaved people in 1777. Slowly, other northern states did too.

Some people had long opposed slavery. Called abolitionists, they were especially active in the 1830s, fighting slavery's injustice with words and sometimes force.

"What, to the American slave, is your Fourth of July?" asked abolitionist Frederick Douglass on July 5, 1852. How can someone who is not free celebrate freedom?

But emancipation stopped cold at the southern states: they refused to free their enslaved people. Enslaved people's work made lots of money for large southern farms, so in these states especially, freedom for all was bad for business.

Abolitionists worked hard to end slavery. But in some states, enslavers (those who held enslaved people) worked just as hard to keep it going.

Although Congressman Abraham Lincoln didn't always believe Black and white people deserved equal rights, he did believe the idea of slavery was wrong. When he was elected president in 1860, seven southern states did the unthinkable and broke away from the United States of America. They left the nation to form a new country called the Confederate States of America, sometimes called the Confederacy, where slavery would remain legal.

On April 12, 1861, the Civil War began, Southern states versus Northern states—Confederacy versus Union.

The North entered the war because they did not want the United States to break up into two countries. However, eventually the war became a battle to end slavery.

As the Civil War continued, President Lincoln took steps to end slavery. On January 1, 1863, he issued an order called the Emancipation Proclamation, declaring all enslaved persons in the now ten states of the Confederacy "forever free." The Thirteenth Amendment to the constitution was passed two years later, after the Civil War ended, officially freeing all enslaved people in the United States.

Slavery had become illegal, but in Confederate Texas, enslavers kept that news a secret.

The big state of Texas was far from where most of the battles of the Civil War were being fought, so no Union soldiers were close enough to make sure the new laws were followed there. Texas farm owners had crops to harvest and sell. Without enslaved workers, who would pick them?

The Civil War had ended, but enslaved Texans were not told the truth. They continued working, because they didn't know they were actually free.

The Confederacy surrendered to the Union on April 9, 1865. But it wasn't until June 19 that Union General Gordon Granger arrived in Galveston, Texas. The war now over, he declared his General Order Number Three from a balcony:

"The people of Texas are informed that, in accordance with a proclamation from the Executive of the United States, all slaves are free . . ."

900 days after the Emancipation Proclamation,

89 years after Independence Day,

339 years after the first enslaved Africans came to the land that is now America,

. . . the secret was *finally* out: Freedom now belongs to enslaved people, too.

Newly freed Texans began to feel the long-delayed warmth of liberty's glow. As the news spread, they prayed, ate, and sang in celebration, though some were still in shock. Others left right away to search for and reunite with long-lost family members from whom they had been separated by slavery.

June 19 became Jubilee Day—it was *their* independence day.

Starting in 1866, families and communities in Texas held the first yearly Jubilee Day celebrations. The next year, the Freedmen's Bureau hosted the first Jubilee Day held in the state capital and taught formerly enslaved people about the privileges that freedom offered them.

Jubilee Day festivities grew as the newly emancipated used their new rights to earn money and purchase property. They bought land and built parks like Emancipation Park in Houston, their own spaces where they could freely gather in their best clothes to barbecue, sing, dance, pray, and play.

At many Jubilee Days, the Emancipation Proclamation was recited so that everyone could reflect on the words that had changed their lives forever.

Jubilee Day became "Juneteenth," short for its date of June 19.

Not all Black people saw Juneteenth as a reason to hold big, joyous events. Some felt their pain from enslavement would never be understood by younger generations who hadn't lived through it, so they hosted their own separate gatherings. Others tried to ignore Juneteenth altogether. Slavery was a terrible memory, and they preferred not to talk about it.

And even though Black people were no longer enslaved, freedom wasn't the same for them as it was for other Americans. As the 1900s arrived, new laws spread throughout the South, limiting Black people's rights and keeping Black and white people separate.

Called Jim Crow laws, these rules made it hard for many Black people to have access to opportunities like good jobs and education. Black people couldn't even enjoy parks where only whites were allowed, forcing many Juneteenth festivities to be held far outside of town.

WHITE ONLY

Between Jim Crow and major events of the early 1900s, like World War I and the Great Depression, Juneteenth began to lose its shine. During World War I, some people considered the celebration not American, a reminder of a sad time not worth talking about. And during the Great Depression of 1929–1939, people didn't have much extra time or money to use to host fairs and parties.

But Juneteenth remained in the hearts of many Black Texans.

In 1936, after years of little attention, sparks of Juneteenth reignited with a momentary bang! The Texas Centennial Exposition welcomed more than 46,000 Black visitors to a huge Juneteenth celebration to open its groundbreaking Hall of Negro Life. An entire building dedicated to famous Black inventors, scholars, celebrities, and more, it featured huge murals illustrating the history of Black Texans. Pride burned in the hearts of everyone who participated.

As time passed, Black people, especially in the South, grew tired of Jim Crow laws casting shadows on their rights. Many moved north and west for better opportunities, and some also worked together to fight back as part of the Civil Rights Movement.

Juneteenth spread as Black Texans moved across America and shared their traditions in their new cities. In the Civil Rights Movement, activists even made Juneteenth part of the 1968 Poor People's Campaign in Washington, DC, a march for fair access to jobs and housing for people without them. More than 50,000 people took part, and many brought Juneteenth with them back to their homes around the country.

In the 1970s, as America prepared to mark 200 years of independence, many Black people remembered Frederick Douglass's words and realized something: their freedom was not 200 years old.

For some, Juneteenth now symbolized their independence day.

In Milwaukee, Wisconsin; Buffalo, New York; and more cities well beyond Texas, new Juneteenth traditions came to life. Families reunited, learned about their heritage, paraded, barbecued, and celebrated together. Their festivals grew larger each year.

In Texas, Juneteenth festivities continued, and some celebrations—like Austin's, which had stopped for twenty-five years—were revived. And more than 110 years after the first Juneteenth, State Representative Al Edwards succeeded in making it an official Texas state holiday in 1979.

Though Juneteenth has long been recognized in many communities, most Americans still didn't know about it or its history. But a series of horrific events in the weeks before Juneteenth 2020, and a resurgence of Black Lives Matter protests in response put a long-overdue spotlight on how poorly Black people have continued to be treated in America.

Those events, and the decades-long efforts of activists and government officials, helped Juneteenth finally start to get the national attention it deserves. On June 17, 2021, over 150 years since the first Jubilee Day, it was made an official American holiday.

Falling just weeks before Independence Day each year, Juneteenth is a time to remember and celebrate our enslaved ancestors' strength and perseverance. But it also reminds us to keep working toward the American dream: liberty and justice for *all*.

EMANCIPATION DAY

Juneteenth is the best-known nationwide celebration of the end of enslavement, though it has Texan roots. However, "Emancipation Day" has been observed on other dates and locally in other states and districts as well (Washington, DC; Florida; Maryland; and others). It coincides with many landmark dates: those states' notification of freedom or their ratification (passing) of legislation outlawing enslavement, the signing of the Thirteenth Amendment, and even the abolition of African enslavement in other regions like the Caribbean.

While Texas was the last state in the Confederacy to notify its enslaved people of their emancipation, slavery was still legal in Union border states Maryland, Missouri, Delaware, and Kentucky until the Thirteenth Amendment was ratified in December 1865.

1526: Spanish enslavers kidnap African people and take them to an attempted colony near what is now Georgia or South Carolina.

January 1, 1863: The Emancipation Proclamation takes effect, with Lincoln using his wartime rights as Commander-in-Chief to free enslaved people in Confederate States.

January 31, 1865: The Thirteenth Amendment is passed by the House of Representatives, making enslavement illegal in the United States.

June 19, 1865: General Gordon Granger arrives in Galveston, Texas, and delivers General Order Number Three, telling enslaved people in Texas of their freedom for the first time.

1936: The federally funded, groundbreaking Hall of Negro Life exhibit draws more than 46,000 Black Texans to celebrate Juneteenth at the Texas Centennial Exposition.

1968: The Poor People's Campaign, led by Ralph David Abernathy and Coretta Scott King after the assassination of Dr. Martin Luther King Jr., uses Juneteenth to close out the campaign.

1976: Buffalo, New York, hosts its first Juneteenth celebration as other celebrations emerge throughout America.

TIMELINE

1619: This is the first known instance of enslaved African people kidnapped from Angola by English enslavers to the English colony Jamestown, in what is now the state of Virginia.

1808: The Act Prohibiting Importation of Slaves of 1807 takes effect, which makes it illegal to transport enslaved people from other nations into the United States.

April 12, 1861 – April 9, 1865: The Civil War divides America.

June 19, 1866: The first Jubilee Day, or Emancipation Day, festivities are held in Texas.

1872: Houston's Emancipation Park is built on land purchased by formerly enslaved residents to be used for Juneteenth celebrations.

Late 1800s: June 19, also known as Jubilee Day or Emancipation Day in Texas, unofficially becomes Juneteenth.

1979: Juneteenth is declared a Texas state holiday, pushed by the efforts of Texas State Representative Al Edwards.

2020: Juneteenth gets the national spotlight as the country witnesses the brutal, race-driven murder of George Floyd at the hands of the police in May 2020, inspiring a surge of Black Lives Matter protests and acknowledgement of the Juneteenth emancipation holiday.

2021: President Joseph Biden signs legislation making Juneteenth a federal holiday, the first federal holiday added to the calendar in nearly forty years.

MY JUNETEENTH CONNECTION

When I was growing up in Buffalo, New York, observing Juneteenth was an annual tradition for me and my family. My hometown has been celebrating this once exclusively Texan holiday since 1976 thanks to the efforts of BUILD, a civil rights organization founded by Black activists in Buffalo.

When America prepared to mark the 200th anniversary of independence in 1976, BUILD's membership recognized that the first Independence Day festivities did not include Black America's enslaved descendants. They had heard of Juneteenth, a Texan emancipation holiday that had been celebrated elsewhere, and decided to adopt this holiday as an additional Independence Day for Black Buffalonians.

One of Juneteenth Festival of Buffalo's co-founders is Judson T. Price Jr., a retired guidance counselor and well-known community leader in our city, who would become a longtime Juneteenth Buffalo board member. I also proudly call him "Papa"—he is my maternal grandfather. He and his co-founders established what would become the third-largest Juneteenth celebration in the country—including the ones held in Texas! While Juneteenth Buffalo was led by its president emeritus Marcus Brown for twenty of its forty-six years, Papa was unofficially dubbed "Mr. Juneteenth" by many. He still often sports a Juneteenth hat or T-shirt; in the early days of the festival, he designed and screen-printed festival gear himself.

Our family and friends have countless memories and photos from Juneteenth festivals over the years—parades, delicious food, concerts, health expos, 5K runs, Underground Railroad tours, and more! As children, my cousin and I were (adorable) members of the Juneteenth royal court, and I later even had a little stand with my family where I sold handmade pencil toppers. One of my favorite Juneteenth archival photos is of my grandmother Frances Price (she and my grandfather were a dynamic duo!) and the iconic rapper Kurtis Blow at a 1980s Juneteenth Buffalo concert. She was talking to him backstage in her familiar stance—one hand on her hip and a finger in the air, typically used for telling someone what they were or weren't supposed to do.

Juneteenth was thrust into the national spotlight in June 2020 during the Black Lives Matter protests following the murder of George Floyd and the triggering racial profiling of Christian Cooper. In 2020, many Americans of *all* colors (yes, even many Black Americans!) learned about this holiday for the first time. Thanks to nearly a half-century of Juneteenth Buffalo's efforts, Juneteenth was nothing new to Buffalonians like me.

But the holiday is still bittersweet. What Juneteenth acknowledges—an over 900-day extension of an already brutal and unjust system—is not lost on many. But we will always be proud of the resilience and miracle of our ancestors' survival through it all.

What's your Juneteenth connection? How will you celebrate?

Brimming with creative inspiration, how-to projects, and useful information to enrich your everyday life, quarto.com is a favorite destination for those pursuing their interests and passions.

This edition published in 2022 by becker&mayer! kids,
an imprint of The Quarto Group,
11120 NE 33rd Place, Suite 201, Bellevue, WA 98004 USA.
(T)+1 425-827-7120 (F) +1 425-828-9659
www.Quarto.com

becker&mayer! kids titles are also available at discount for retail, wholesale, promotional, and bulk purchase. For details, contact the Special Sales Manager by email at specialsales@quarto.com or by mail at The Quarto Group, Attn: Special Sales Manager, 100 Cummings Center Suite 265D, Beverly, MA 01915 USA.

22 23 24 25 26   5 4 3

ISBN: 978-0-7603-7514-3

Printed in USA

Editor's note: The map on pages 6 and 7 references a general map of the United States from 1857, showing the area and extent of the free and slave-holding states, and the territories of the Union, as well as the boundary of the seceding states. **Source:** https://www.loc.gov/resource/g3701e.cw1020000/